D1624316

BOA
EDITIONS
LIMITED

THE HEAT OF ARRIVALS

Poems by
Ray Gonzalez

BOA Editions, Ltd. ⌣ Brockport, NY ⌣ 1996

LC #: 96-83947
ISBN: 1–880238–38–1 cloth
ISBN: 1–880238–39–X paper

First Edition
96 97 98 99   7 6 5 4 3 2 1

Publications by BOA Editions, Ltd.—
a not-for-profit corporation under section 501 (c) (3)
of the United States Internal Revenue Code—
are made possible with the assistance of grants from
the Literature Program of the New York State Council on the Arts,
and the Literature Program of the National Endowment for the Arts,
the Lannan Foundation,
as well as from the Rochester Area Foundation Community Arts Fund
administered by the Arts & Cultural Council for Greater Rochester,
the County of Monroe, NY,
and from many individual supporters.

Cover Art: "El Sol Nativo / The Native Sun," by Pedro Romero,
Courtesy of Red Crane Books
Cover Design: Geri McCormick
Author Photo: Gary Isaacs
Typesetting: Richard Foerster
Manufacturing: McNaughton & Gunn, Lithographers
BOA Logo: Mirko

BOA Editions, Ltd.
A. Poulin, Jr., President
92 Park Avenue
Brockport, NY 14420

This book is for the late Arturo Islas
who finally went home to
the Franklin Mountains of Del Sapo

Contents

III. The Energy of Clay

IV. The Heat of Arrivals

THE HEAT OF ARRIVALS

I.
In the Time of the Scorpion

Watching a Film About Van Gogh
on Christmas Eve

The madness of the ear listening
to the silence of the sunflowers
makes us wait for Christmas to pass
so we can return our gifts,

smear our hands and faces with paint,
go beyond the memory of the crude angel
wanting freedom impossible on canvas.

*

Van Gogh scrawls "I am the whole spirit"
on his studio wall, screams
as he drinks the turpentine,
yells for his brother Theo

who exhibits paintings to a world
that doesn't know the creator buys time
with canvas nailed to the broken wood,
frames he rips as he stumbles in a field of crows.

*

Days ago I was asked by someone to speak
on the difference between spirit and soul.
I had myself photographed,
the picture revealing too much,
its light separating white from black.

It shows a man standing without his glasses,
wondering why the photographer chose
my bare features few have seen,
a profile emerging out of a negative

with the artist's chemical burning
brown skin upon my blinded face.

★

Van Gogh tears sunflowers off their stalks,
kicks the canvas, staggers across the horizon
to find himself in front of the mirror,
blue and yellow paint coagulating on his lips.
He tastes the brush, then screams into
the mirror of comprehension as he slices his ear.

★

Hymns rise when we recall
where we were on this night years ago.
We ate bread for the birth that exhausts
our beliefs in getting there.

It is our swallowing of the paint in secret,
washing our mouths and hands,
until we are empty on Christmas Eve,
yet filled with a yearning we ignored for years.

We wait for something to happen—
a photo to reveal the instant the camera clicked
and the crows vanished in the sunflowers,
returned the canvas to dirt.

We shredded it as we dived into
Van Gogh's mirror of Christmas stars
and never came back,
the abandoned yellow field proof
this is the difference between spirit and soul.

Black Ink Drawings

I worked on them for two decades,
intricate drawings swallowing   every second I breathed,
tiny ink squares falling against my eyesight,
containing whole villages in their white space,
indecipherable cemeteries and crosses,
hieroglyphics deciphered   for those who won't speak
as they mark their own graffiti.

These drawings formed a message
for the black and blue ink man,
the motes of letter and pen,
an artist who took three months to fill
one square inch of yellowed paper.
One sketch is stained   with the air of flight,
the doubling over of the earth in the days
when we traced the smoldering glaze
that contained versions   of daybreak.

The circles I drew never changed color,
punishment for   my wrinkled hands,
strain upon my eyes when I followed
the red ink I hesitated to use.
Another drawing demanded I trace its line
as the sketch   of red distortions,
scribbles cut in the page when I saw
the blue horse seed   into black nostrils
of the face I could never draw.

I have scratched on the page for years,
let my hand go wherever,
angular incitations   crisscrossing
as the codes rewritten for
          the overlooked faces,
removed from the caves

as secret work   terrible sights
from the white fields emerging in black,
the color we understand
when we cut the surface for years,
draw with the quill we brand
upon the books of our own greed.

The Manuscripts

*"The manuscript now is nothing but a calendar calculating
the shortest routes to the stone."*
        —Arkadii Dragomoschenko

You seek the hardest surface
to show how far you have gone after
rolling down the cliff,

yucca that marked you with a blood puzzle
you carried like a blossom on your back,
search to find the shortest path to the tablets,

unmistakably sad dreams
that wake you early
and make you sleep late.

When you rise from the lines of the etchings,
you wipe your work and begin again,
enter the passage where you left

the broken slabs to disintegrate
into words of the emperor
you will never be allowed to have.

The manuscripts fall short of answers.
You walk barefoot beyond the quotes,
wish for a time when you know

how to divide yourself into two people—
the one who sits quietly
and listens to the insect nestled in his palm,

and the one who takes the chisel,
pauses before the food of heaven,
and betrays everything he has learned.

The Eagles in the Ashes

A Dream

Walking down the alley toward
my grandmother's house where I grew up,
I see trees, lawns and houses in the barrio
breathing a fine layer of ashes,
mounds of gray powder piled
against the torn fence.

Five giant eagles rise out of it,
enormous birds with brown faces
of long-haired, silent men.
Without flapping their wings,
they step down the mound,
strong-taloned feet sinking
in the fine dust.

Each eagle walks past me
without saying a word,
their long, black hair swirling,
bronze faces proud and knowing,
feathers shining in the ashes.

They jump onto the wire fence,
then land in the yard.
One by one, they walk into
my grandmother's house.
I stand by the gate,
sift ashes through my fingers,
rub my hands together
before climbing the mound,
trying to get over the fence,
slipping down and getting up,
trying to open the gate.

Watering My Chinese Elm

For Ida

A black butterfly hurtles out of its leaves
as I turn the sprinkler,
its wings brushing my head
in surprise the tree survives,
its bed of white flowers surrounding
the hole I dug, the spot I chose to plant
my first real marriage tree.

Watering its thin trunk, I think of the mountain man
approaching the high lake,
parting branches from his face,
becoming a priest of fish,
abandoning the peaks to care for his elms,
collecting the black lines in their skin
and sitting by the lake to toss his desire
into water that reaches for him.

Moving the hose, I startle a gray moth out of the grass,
out of the reach of the priest.
It lay hidden under the tree as the folded parchment
containing truths I told the one I loved,
wings rapid as the mountain man grabbing hold
of the last twig before giving in.

The moth's awkward flight begins in the grass
as I water my elm for tomorrow's footprints,
form green leaves for deciphering truths,
help the tree in its growth
as it takes over the yard,
its spreading branches keeping me
farther back from its pale bark.

Pollen Paintings

Made from crushed petals of flowers,
           the pollen is dropped on the sand to reveal
the vision of the man opening his hands
           to let the powders fall.
The grains land in a random pattern,
           form the intaglio of the sun and the wish,
symbols discovered by the grandfather
           who died without speaking last words to his grandson.
He was the father who told him pollen and petals
           are the honeyed eyes that will help him see
           what is going to happen to him.

The man with the sticky hands sees
           the blue, orange, and green on his fingers,
the colored sand taking shape,
           its sweet aura of the open and closed fist.
He knows it is the creation of the finger
           tracing his death upon the brown horizon
as the wind rearranges everything.
His hands drop more pollen because
           it is the dust of gravity, each grain lifting
           his head and arms.

Colors fall and he sees the design will never fade.
           It holds the boundaries of sand
like a flower growing from his fingers,
           the spot where the cells of the mountains
bring their soily light.
           When he runs out of colors,
he follows those who taught him
           to open his hands and drop the grains,
older pollen spreading over
           the breathing canvas of ground.

In the Time of the Scorpion

I found the scorpion crawling near my foot
and knew it was time to die,
fresh out of high school in June,

my room in my parent's house the only place
I could write my first poems,
the scorpion the only visitor I had at night.

I brushed it away from my foot with a pencil
and it sprang for the wall.
I turned off the lamp to light a candle,
its flickering motion spreading to the scorpion.

I stepped closer, watched it become
a drop on the wall,
bloodstain of a long future,
its erect tail poised to sting the clear vision

I had back then, at the age of seventeen,
the power of the scorpion I touched with my pencil,
a flash I could never recapture
in another twenty-five years of poems.

*

I still know the scorpion and descend
into the tears on my back
where the scorpion hits.

When I know the scorpion,
it breathes under my skin,
shows me where to lie down,
wait for its dozen babies to emerge
from the tips of the night thorns.

*

The scorpion came apart under the knife.
I saw the wheel of poison grow into the drop
we would love to smear into our eyes,
be able to see where it came from,

where we started,
anoint our eyes with whatever survives,
bitter our fingertips for the root and the spring.

I saw the sharp, yellow globe emerge to spill
over the torn body and endless legs,
coat it with desire to fight back,

yellow oozing over my blade
like the human face growing
on the dying scorpion.

*

The myth of the scorpion comes to me
to catch the storm over my skin,
fly with the fast creature,

trail under the rocks to wait,
to lift the stone and take a chance,
pick up the stick to spell my bite in the sand.

I go back to the old house and enter
the room, find the screen on the window still there,
hardened drops on the wire proving
the myth scorpions glow in the dark.

*

The time of the scorpion is near.
Humidity no longer hides its form
in the black corners of the room,
signals the summer of being stung that night.

My blood refused to come out.
I knew how to take the red scorpion,
find what it was like to go down,
jump out of the way
of the wetness inside.

Salamander

Its transparent skin a membrane of confession,
brown spots on the window screen like a puzzle.
Its webbed feet clutch the wire
as if letting go meant evolution went wrong.
I could lift it onto my finger,
hope it was the answer,
let it cling like a twig in its path.

I wait for it to open its mouth,
so I can quit thinking it is an omen—
the underground stream, at last, ignited,
or my flesh unrecognized in a new country.
It could be the carrier of the sweat and smoke
I lost when I ran across the border.

It is old desire coming alive,
makes me close the window
before other speckled faces blink at me,
their quickness the fastest way
of letting me know I must be wrong.

Song for the Lizard Painted on the Plate

It circles its tail in blue and black,
trapped in the axis of decoration

like the lizard at my feet
that shot across my body

to warn me I killed too many
of its kind as a boy,

collected their tails in a matchbox
as they fell off on their own.

The lizard painted on the white plate
grows darker each year,

disappears into tumbleweeds
to emerge resting on my chest,

neck pulsing with
its red head turned to me,

furious eyes staring from
wells where I have been.

It wonders how I can lie still
as I burn slowly under the weight of its tail,

sleep to wake alone and find one black bead
of moisture centered on my naked chest.

Indian Petroglyphs, Red Desert, Wyoming

Years without going near any carvings,
my approach toward the red walls a sudden urge
to fall back without getting closer,
without allowing the wind to shave
                    another hundred years off the horse.
Arrows, antelopes, a lone buffalo etched
into the stone face so the desert remains as it is,
a massive break against the prophets
who said it would crumble,
                    a hard ceremony miles from nowhere,
a few feet from the symbols of the soil,
images crackling out of the rocks,
mesquite bushes hiding knives
and campfires from the dusty moon.

Bear paws on the slabs hurtle their claws
through the transparent bodies of eternal wanderers
who etched stories before anyone could stop them
                    from telling the whole tale,
cutting into the mountain to search for the fourth hole,
the coldest point of light that burns
through solid rock, covering the boulders
with hard lines of the painter,
the touch of the one who kisses
hot stone to add to the sun,
who climbs to carve something
                    no one finds for centuries—
a fire, a bird, another bear claw,
the horns of shaking masks,
an unknown, four-legged creature
whose giant mane flies toward
the red arms of the hunter,
mute speech of the first interpreter.

The Mummy in the Witte Museum

Most of his teeth remain.
He grins at the faces
staring down at him over the years,
as if it is time to sit up and embrace them all,
scare them away from the shape in the glass,
move them to want the red necklace
without knowing how many have died wearing it.

> The ugliest things are his feet,
> toes pointing toward the glass
> because it is the way out before the crowd realizes
> the bad luck of air encased with the mummy.
> The shrunken toes curl when he moves
> like the toes of any man who thought he was saved.

The wrapped face moves an eye,
raises and lowers his chest.
Broken hands warn us
not everything stays trapped or recorded.

> He bends a knee without being seen
> by whispering faces who swear it is petrified,
> any movement belonging to their fleeing minds,
> any fear coming out of their own unraveling.

The Olmec Hunchback

The huge stone hump has weighed him down for centuries,
given him reason to erode in museums
as the creator of the petrified chants,

wondering what he did to fall
deformed from the other civilization,
oblong face stretching his forehead to the ground.

His open hands catch a heavier load of rock
against those who excavated him,
displayed him for those who want to go back.

He rubs off the last traces of white dirt
as he comes out of the womb,
the hunchback who hurt his mother

because she had no choice and screamed,
named him as the god who carries the ball of bone
as the center of wisdom no one deserves.

The knot on his back is the cluster of blood and nerve
the old ones talked about when they were afraid—
a curved back of sexual power found in the ground,

his sculpted beauty the last artifact
from a galaxy where the hump is the moon
worshipped at the top of the pyramid.

Black Stone Sculpture

Statue of a naked man sitting,
playing his stone harp,
the round, bald face gasping up at the sky,
the harp standing between his legs.
His ankles are ringed with deep blue bands
of the rock man who sits and plays,
his hands combing the harp
to call the black stone woman
to sit by his side.

Given to me as a gift,
the statue's box was torn open
by burglars in our home before Christmas.
The musician was not taken,
but thrown upside down, triangles and circles
carved on his back by the Mexican artist,
saving his fall.
They are symbols that would come to me
to be deciphered, as someone warned.

I sat him back up without a clue,
his legs spread and pointing
when I put the harp in his hands,
studied his black insect eyes
in the silence of our shock.
I waited for him to come alive
and play a scale for the blessed home,
pluck a string to call
for more stone guardians to appear,
have them sit somewhere with instruments
behind our locked doors.

In Peru, the Quechans Have a Thousand Words for Potato

I hold my cut finger to the ice water,
return from the source of grain in the teeth—
the country where I knew a thousand words for love,

a handful of eye movements, not knowing
which direction to take, which roots to dig
and pile among vegetables.

In Peru, they open their hands,
offer the potato as the fruit from the top of the world,
people who fled the mountains for a crop at lower depths,

descending to cut the potato and find
the white meat, fiber tasting like the grain
that gave them speech.

Their vowels make me wish
I had a thousand words for my body,
a vegetable and tree planted from the testicle,

the black spot in the potato named
for the thousand sons, limbs holding up
the back of the tired worker,

strangers who eat with their fingers and go back
to the high fields for the potato given
the thousand and one name,

dug from the soil they slept on,
the field where they paused to piss
before climbing up the mountain.

Sueño de Mexico

After a painting by Jose Clemente Orozco 1926

Cortes y La Malinche

A dead body at their feet,
Cortes y la Malinche sit up naked
after fucking for the third time.
She sits with eyes closed,
long black hair braided behind her,
large nipples brushed by
the conquistador's right arm.
Cortes shields her against death,
pushes her dark-red body onto the bed.

He stands tall and pale,
heavy legs stepping over the dead body
of a man who couldn't reach them.
Cortes creates the first mestizo of the new world.
No one knows why he chose her
as he thrusts into the first woman,
the latest earthquake rumbling
across the temple when he grunts
and believes everything is settled.

Juarez

Once, stumbling drunk in the mercado of Juarez,
I saw the young whore emerge
from behind the vegetable crates.
She seemed to be in a heroin daze,
emerging from a customer's rape.
Her eyelids were painted in
black mascara to match
black lipstick on her mouth.

She motioned to me to stop,
black fingernails pointing at me
in the stinking tomatoes and goat meat
of the busy mercado.

I moved back, stared at the turistas
who pushed her so they could get
to the bargain of leather belts.
I kept walking toward the bridge,
but couldn't forget the sight of her
long, blonde hair standing up
when she fell to her knees.

I reached the crossing as she reminded me
of the straw doll I found floating
in the Rio Grande long ago.
I made it to the bridge,
recalled how I tossed the doll back,
its warped wood sliding through
my fingers like the young whore
disappearing in my haste to get away.

Cathedral

I climbed the ancient tower
of the cathedral of La Virgin de Guadalupe,
the oldest church in Juarez.
I wanted the myth to be true.
It said if you opened the south window,
you would face the spot on the mountain
where the padres buried the gold.

I climbed the suffocating, wooden stairs,
narrow rock chamber going straight up,
creaking under my weight,
three-hundred year old stones
smelling of forgiven sins.
I climbed to answer the dare

of my high school friends who waited
in the quiet sanctuary below,
trying not to draw attention,
three of us drinking and wandering
around the crowded plaza.

I reached the top, pushed
wooden shutters open to the heavy air.
I stared at the mountains of El Paso miles away,
as if I knew where to look,
spotted a gleam of light in the distance,
so I could be the one to tell my friends
where we should dig for treasure.
I turned around, dizzy, breathing hard,
the confining cell forcing me back.

An old woman stood there,
tight against the railing,
her thin figure draped in dirty rags,
gray hair falling beyond the stairs,
covering a face she wouldn't show.
I looked again and she was gone,
but could smell her presence,
taste the difference in the swallowing air.

I almost fell down the stairs,
got down to find my friends gone.
I made it to the bridge alone,
lost for a few blocks, knowing
the woman in the tower followed me,
nudged me as I reached the check point,
her invisibility marking the last time
I would cross, the beam
on the mountain I would forget
because there were others who had seen
the flame from up there.

Homage to Lucian Blaga

Romanian poet Lucian Blaga was awarded the 1959 Nobel Prize, but his country's totalitarian government kept him from ever accepting it.

"Be glad on the blossom and understand we don't have to know now who brings and spreads fire."
—Lucian Blaga

Brief Beginning

We know the flame kisses
what we believe in.

We take the mystery of invasion
against the great burning,

find a way to guess what
presence breathes fire,

which companion
shares water.

We hold the match to the finger,
paint a change of skin upon ourselves

as punishment for not knowing when to strike,
this branding the way of learning

the language of smoke,
the heat of arrivals.

Heaven and Earth

"Astir under the trees God makes himself smaller to give the red mushrooms room to grow under his bark"

—L. B.

He lies down to fill the earth with poison.
He is under the leaves exciting
the ground to stand erect,
red mushrooms pushing through to spit
at him like tiny demons escaping
the embrace of a god they never thought
would come down for them.

Fate

"In sleep my blood draws me back into my parents like a wave"

— L. B.

Entering their bodies,
I see why it happened this way,
recall the first words I cried,
seconds after my birth,
their sound an incoherent message
for them to let go, leave me,
let me come out to wait for a reply
and grow the way I should have gone,
make it through this passage
without having to look back
at their hesitation, postponement,
desire, and consummation—
without having to take the wrong turn
into the belly of their soul.

Asking

> *"Look, the stars are coming into the world at the same time as my sorrowful questions."*
>
> —L.B.

How far do they travel before
we wish they would explode?
When was the last time we spoke
the instant a falling star streaked
over our heads?
How much do they have to reveal
without using their light?
Who taught the ancestor to look
into the moving ground,
before discovering the nervous sky?

Who decides stars have something more
than their burning sign?
Why do we continue to overlook the comet?
Where do they go after we see?
How many children woke ignoring
the path of their falling hair?

How can we trust the universe
when it expands without us?
Why do we insist on looking up
when the river comes out of our feet?
What does sorrow have to do
with the oncoming mass of radiating whispers?

Without Regret

> *"How humbly bends the arrogant forehead of yesterday's*
> *ecstasy"*
>
> —L.B.

Last night we gave each other everything,
clutched each other to forgive,
couldn't catch our breath,
or follow each other
to the peak of our breasts.

We hurried through love to reach
the morning as one body,
gave up identity for ecstasy,
allowed the naked body to find out,
a flesh-driven need to escape from desire
so we could face our fall
before the silent creator—
the moist surface of marriage
that rewards the lovers who roll
into its vast reach.

Back

> *"I stand turned toward my country—return is a dream*
> *I can't wake from."*
>
> —L.B.

I am constantly going back
across the border where the river fell,
dried before me as a great canyon
opening toward the frontier.

My nameless country is where I settled
as the man who got this far
by turning his back on mountains
who first greeted the child before

cutting red forests into the clouds.

I can't wake from this scene
of coming back to see
if desert rains tore open everything,
revisit old adobe where I was given answers—
words cut into the walls like maps carved
by those preceding me into sleep,

the moment when I fell into the muddy water
upon finding myself at home, about to wake up.

II.
The Snake Poems

The Sustenance

"I inhabit a sacred wound.
I inhabit imaginary ancestors."
                    —Aimé Césaire

Campesinos bend in the 115 degree heat,
dig the holes and disappear
when the family comes north
to build the desert railroads.
My grandparents, Julia y Bonifacio, married at fourteen
to escape *la revolucion* for Arizona railroad camps
where Yaqui Indians laid the tracks.
Special teams walked ahead to clear
the line of five-foot rattlesnakes,
dozens of them slowing the tracks,
taking out a worker here and there,
defying the cuts in the arroyos,
workers killing and bagging them,
living on snake meat to get across the Sonora.

Bonifacio, the foreman, refused snake meat,
packing beans and tortillas Julia made.
Once, he had to bite into the fried meat
fresh out of the campfire.
He burned his mouth, "Cabron! Chingaw!"
He threw the meat into the dirt
as the silent workers stared at him,
wondered if he knew it was bad luck to waste
what the land gave to them.

The tossed meat dried into a greasy spot,
attracted flies and ants in the sand,
even the buzzard hovering after the tracks
had grown ten miles down the line,
rattlers crawling out when the sun went down—
thick giants overlooked in the path of progress,

the railroad crew unaware the spoiled meat would wash away
in the rains that fell, flooded everything
that unforgettable Christmas, 1941,
three days after Bonifacio dropped of a heart attack.

Black Adobe

I go to the adobe house,
regress into the snake boy I've hated,
forgiven his coiling across rooms,
shedding of his skin.
I enter through the cracks,
feel the cool water in the clay jars
where an old rattler laid its eggs
to harden the foundation,
kept it from crumbling.

      My hands push against mud.
      I open my eyes.
      The lone table and clay jar wait
      to be carried away.
      I wonder why there are no black tortillas
      to slap in my hands.
      I smell them, the odor
      cracking the corners
      where the snake waits
      to dance on the working fingers.

I clean the house,
but can't do anything about the dirt floor
pulling my bare feet to stand still.
I wait for the snake, secretly lodged there
since my grandmother told me
I would enter and be taken into the dwelling
that tears open the fang.

Eating the Snake

The tongue, a starving messenger,
does not fear the taste.
It closes around the hot meal,
a gulp in the stomach
that survives knowing the reptile.

The stomach grows from the seed.
It is accustomed to the jalapeño,
skin peeling back to share
the flame and strike,
add flavor to the snake that nourishes
each mouthful we take.

The reptile is a secret.
It spoke before we could speak.
It gave in to the venom and the hunt.
Eating the snake from under the rock
is the only thing left to recite.
Cutting the snake from under the heart
is our way of talking without the tongue.

The Blue Snake

I stand in the reptile house,
look for the blue snake that calls me
to join it on display,
amuse us by spitting at
strangers who love snakes.

I walk over the tiled passageway
in search of the diamondback
I hacked as a boy, slicing it
with the shovel I carried,
watched it become the blue snake.

I curl up the tree, wait to be fed,
too wise to hunt the frog,
preferring the rat in the cage,
the meal coming to me,
afraid I will miss it if I move
too far into the trees.
I pass the locked doors into the glass
where the blue snake waits hungry,
yet fed, alive but unseen,
still not found by me.

I leave after searching each stall.
The boa and copperhead have a long way to go
before turning blue, neither one knowing me
when I killed blue lightning
to prevent a storm of open flesh,
drove metal through the ground,
my wonder over the clean pieces
sending the snake on its way
before I could enter the glass,
find the hidden eyes sparkling off the wire
where the rattle keeps missing a beat for me.

The Rattle

I hear it often,
look down to search   for the instrument
of the hand and the wrist,
the rattle   of warning,
instrument of the foot   and the body.

I hear it again,
erect drum   hidden in mesquite,
a rapid ear song for those
                    who step the other way,
chant for the wrong reason.

I hear it in my breath,
see the cut-off rattle   drying in the sun,
a snake bent   to the fate
of the one who was bitten
                    to inherit the dance.

I hear it across the miles
of arid land,
listen for   the shaking
to interpret one footstep
set down   on the harvested plain.

I don't want it
to go away,   wait to see
how close I get to
the transparent layers   of rattle
containing every   third eye
I closed and put away.

The Snake in Winter

It reminds me of things I have lost,
how they lie underground,

wait for the next man
to find them.

One of those men once told me
about blowing up

the hibernating rattlers
with dynamite in winter,

dropping the charges
into the rocks

to sing them awake,
the explosion hurtling

pieces of snake
across the arroyo,

snow collapsing like
the thousand blind faces

of people we loved and left,
memories flying

as fleshy projectiles
humming and spraying

their names over
our wet, bloody heads.

I Knew Who I Was Before I Dreamed
of the Snake

I see through the boulder.
It shows me the mountain lion coming down.

I see the hole in the ground.

It moves with dozens of rattlers
no one believes I have ever seen.

I knew who I was before I was encircled
by instinct and the window my parents gave me.

I knew how to milk the snake
and steal the venom.

I see through the window.
It stands for the anger in the story,

a hard tunnel to the outside.

I know what lies in the cool grass
and how it got there.

I knew who I was before I dreamed of the snake
that inhabited my happiness

and took my fear away.

I saw it again when I opened my eyes,
the first to wake and handle it with bare hands.

Rattlesnake Dance, Coronado Hills, 1966

After the photo "Hopi Snake Dance" by Edward Curtis

Snakes in the mouth.
From the ground to the mouth, to the sky,
dancers curl in a circle to gather snakes,
carry them in their mouths.

They dance for rain,
faces painted like blind snakes
of the first born, the ones that can't see,
yet sense where the heart moves,
where to strike after the rain dance.

*

I climb up the steep arroyo,
listen for the rattle and buzz,
a boy of fourteen looking for the rattler
I spotted the day before.
Its quickness behind the rocks becomes
a stillness along the dirt walls,
a sign there is nothing there,
until I trip and roll a few yards down,
laughing, calling to my friends to come up,
not knowing they ran when they heard it
because I climbed too far.

*

Women and children watch the dance from the high walls.
Only the men can gather the snakes in their arms and mouths.
Only the men can pick them up and wear them
like new arms and legs coming rapidly alive,
quick appendages crawling into the body to make it whole.

I found it nailed to the wooden fence,
the rattle cut off, its skin peeled back
and left hanging in the breeze.
Stiff patterns blew like paper
with an unknown alphabet burned in blood.
The killer left the skin as a god exposing
the fate of snakes to those who follow them.

The flat, wrinkled head dripped,
its beauty crushed into the wood,
its pure instinct beaten back
before it could kiss the follower,
brand him with the wisdom that fire,
someday, must enter the body,
wash it of desire and breath,
swell it to the size of dying,
shape it into a form this one can't take
as I pull it off the fence.

One dancer bends over,
grabs two rattlers in one hand,
his grace in the sun a stain in the photo,
his disappearance in the moving circle
a sign the snakes coiled into the bone of song
like muscles given and granted,
flutes of rain spitting at the red sky that falls
around the tight chests of the exhausted men.

After killing three of them,
I saw the fourth climb up the porch,
squeeze into the bricks to disappear
into a corner of the house.

Its sleek body vanished into the wall,
become a part of our home.

I never saw it again, but lay awake at night,
knowing it was inside the house,
trapped between wood and mortar,
moving from room to room without rattling.
It waited for me to press my hands
above my bed, push in the dark,
tap and push the wall that smothered
every breath I took as I waited.

★

The dancers run and chant, faster and faster,
dozens of snakes crossing their feet,
falling off painted bodies,
blending into the hair and masks,
clinging to their necks as the dancers hold each other.

The circle grows smaller as snakes fly through legs,
women and children staring from above,
the pit of dancers growing deeper,
the round floor of the earth collapsing
to let men and snakes go their way,
choose movements for hiding or revealing
how much blood to let per beat,
how much blood per rattle,
to spit into the starting rain.

Three Snakes, Strawberry Canyon, Berkeley

For Phil Woods

The Rattlesnake

We really didn't see it,
the guy walking ahead of us
saying it struck and missed him.
He pointed to the tall grass.
"If you get closer, you can see its eyes."
We looked, but didn't see it and kept walking.
I thought about those rattlers I killed as a boy,
the nest of six baby rattlers we found in the yard,
my mother insisting I kill them,
saying the babies were more lethal
because they could fill you with venom,
not knowing when to pull back like adult snakes.
I recalled how I killed them
and wanted this rattler to bite the hiker,
so I could forget his bravery and his wonder.

The Garter Snake

It looked like an overgrown worm,
tiny and quick as it flashed across the trail,
its sidewinding motion leaving marks in the dirt.
As we noticed it, we forgot what we said about poetry,
how those things vanish, then reappear before us,
how we admit black and green bands of the garter snake
are the same colors we miss when we write anything.

The Gopher Snake

We found it sleeping in the middle of the trail.
It didn't move, but sparkled as we approached.
It wasn't the rattler that haunts me.
This snake looked like a giant slug,
a slow, wet creature sunning itself.
Suddenly, we admitted it was good luck
to have snakes cross our path
like unknown pulses traveling underground,
ahead of us, all the way to the bottom
of the surprising, moving canyon.

Snakes as a Gift for My Aching Shoulder

I saw a rattlesnake eaten by another rattler.

*

I saw an egg break open,
the yoke of eternity, the liquid
pouring heat on my injured shoulder,
             a snake coiling its muscle into mine,
my shoulder blade a shield
against the striking head.

*

The snake coils
as if this circle
         empowers it
            to take me away from
the den in volcanic rock,
              beckoning
my closed eyes to drop
into the eggs.

*

One snake belongs in the tree.
           One snake fills the flower on the *ocotillo*
to form a pollen that spread
a trust in what
        comes out of the ground.

*

A snake swims into the hole
where I built a fort of sand,
          its low walls protecting me
from the hidden white lake
          about to shower me with venom.

*

A snake devoured a shoe.
I wanted it to contain
          my foot.

*

I saw the erect rattle
inside the skull of salt.
I saw it rattle,
then I heard the beat pass through
          the nerve I tore
when I started believing.

*

The body meets the soul
          as it sheds its skin,
leaves it clinging on a low branch.
A slight breeze rustles it
as I touch
          the brittle designs,
think of the thief
with nothing to steal.

*

The fang disappears
                    in the cake of flesh,
recalls how I first recognized a rattler
by entering the canyon at birth,
tried to open my eyes
                    without the slithering umbilical,
                         harsh rope of holding onto
the seed that shaped the fang.

The Grandfather

The grandfather goes down to the lanterns
and lights the stars.

He takes his bottle and recalls the rattler
he killed to make way for the family.

The grandfather shaves in the morning,
cuts his throat at night.

The blossom of what he knows
spills against the years of healing,

of going down
to the railroad lanterns

to light his aching arms and legs
with the ointment of his scars.

Snakeskin

I thought the rattler was dead
and I stuck my finger in its mouth,
felt the fangs bite down,
penetrate me without letting go,
the fire removing my eyes,
replacing them with green light
of the reptile illuminating my hand.

It entered my bone and blood,
until my whole body was green and damp,
my whole left side turning
slick and cool as I tried
to pull it out of my body.

I peeled my skin back to find
my veins were green and held
tightly what I believed,
what forced itself into me,
what I allowed to be given
without knowing I carried that secret,

crawled over the ground,
became sinew the sun steps on.
I leaned against a huge boulder,
sweated, waited, slept,
and, by morning, found a new way
of embracing that rock,
new life in the green flesh of the world.

III.
The Energy of Clay

The Past

I quit depending on the smell of the earth
to give me an idea about what was there,
what happened, how I could read
          the marks in the arroyos to pronounce
the ones that became mouths
to startle villages,
as if the world knew how to take me apart
and call me by my name.

*

If I am haunted by my past,
I don't know how to get rid
of the beggar in the mercado
who tried to trip me
as I walked by lost, trying to find
my way back to El Paso.

He whispers in my ear,
          holds out his dirty foot to press it
into the small of my back, drag me down
to tell me I can't return without
remembering every lost friend,
river, or mountain.

When I make it home,
buildings are spray-painted with welcoming letters
written by young boys who don't know
what I did yesterday,
how I was able to read their words
          without accusing them of loss.

I tell them about the Arizona shadows
of my grandfather, my mother admitting
she lay on his deathbed as a little girl,

watched the blood drip out
of his mouth as he died.

I write with the melting candle,
try to interpret the falling wax
that drips and says
I will move from my past
the day and night I am able to say,
"This is how it happened.
This is how it happens.
This is how it is going to be."

Memory of the Hand

The hand recalls what it has held,
the fist of truth wedged inside the knuckles,

fitting into the drum of things you cared about,
lifting its memory to allow you

to be alone when
you are not alone,

forcing you to reach out, take care
of things you created with your hands,

taking your father's arm
you have never held,

helping him cross the street
where you let him go

without waving goodbye or making
a fist at him in anger.

The hand aches for what it has held,
mist washing its fingers like a smoke

where you hid knowledge of a sign language,
a movement of joints,

palms and fingers trying to spell
the silent moment when

you touched what moved out
of your reach—

a soft yearning, a bare back,
the tiny mountain range of spine rising

to remind you the hand holds onto little flesh,
knows nothing about the skin except lines

on its own palm, deep furrows where
the weight of remembrance is held.

The Cathedral of My Father

It towers in our country
I abandoned as a child,

its bells tolling for mourners
who never go away,

its foundation fading when I enter
its heavy, wooden doors,

go into the cathedral to wipe
the ashes off my forehead

like holy water that has blessed
too many ghosts,

scent of candles and incense drifting
above the prone body of my father,

lying by the altar, waiting for me
to admit he died at a great distance,

and I never knew if he was coming
or going toward me when he stepped

into the candle light
to set the church on fire.

How?

"We were told that bodies rising to heaven lose their vulvas, their ovaries, wombs, that her body in resurrection becomes a male body."

—Susan Griffin

She died and did not become a male,
but a memory following me
when I thought I knew something about women
when all I had was the father who never spoke
because his mother died and went to heaven
when he was five, her vulva cutting his tongue
to cast it into a cloud of ovaries hovering
over her quiet son.

She died and he became a man of the street,
could never speak to his son
because you must be punished
for losing the mother so young.
She died and never cut the umbilical cord
until she crashed into the hidden life,
the fist her son carried in his groin when
he fathered a son, wanting other bodies to

obey him when he turned his back on his family,
his boys and girls confusing sex
with the natural shame of the earth,
because mothers told them
not to gaze at the water
that opens the wombs of a long life,
its silent answers and its mute sons.

Four Times the Feast

The Vapor of Calling

He is the father without a job,
having lost everything after years
of diamond rings, Cadillac cars,
and the woman of the street.
He visits my ill sister, sits
in her living room a broken man
who no longer responds to her paintings,
watercolors dripping toward
the flesh of creative starvation.

Beans and Tortillas

The smell of beans and tortillas covers me
like the blanket my grandmother made
for my throbbing legs the year I fell
and was confined to bed,
fed by the hot bowl of bean and tortillas
where my finger first rubbed
one letter of the alphabet,
traced it in the brown juice
at the bottom of the bowl,
sopped it up with the last piece of tortilla
before I spilled it on the bed,
covered my head with the warm blanket.

Habaneros

Bright orange peppers crossbred from
the seeds of Mayan soil, brought north to hurt
in the mouths of those who bite to keep going,
who sweat and hallucinate with this new breed of chile.

It melts the top of our heads, brings back
the great jalapeño fields where I stumbled as a boy,
saw the landscape had nothing to do
with my burnt-black tongue.
I called my sisters when I wanted to play or fight,
allowing the smoke of the tongue to escape
because the stem of the habanero was the vine of thought.

Hunger

My sister starves herself in delayed response.
She waits for my father to visit
after years of staying away, our parents' divorce
starving its own memory.
My sister refuses to eat,
weighs eighty pounds while I have dieted,
lost fifty pounds to be able to breathe
and listen to my heart cry out from
the deep fat that protected me
from the love and hate of others,
as I waited for a bigger meal
my family could eat together.
I lose weight now, sit alone and eat my vegetables,
reduce the distance between the lean and the fat,
the starving and the full,
the ones who don't eat because swallowing
would mean a table full of empty bowls,
a stomach murmuring that we are going to forget.

Without

Which of my deeds was done against my will?
How often did I come from   the grasshopper in the forehead
to admit I never embraced my mother?

Who belongs sitting at my collection of tables,
drinking water I never poured?
The beehive in the body   must never be seen.

The dragon is my grandfather who built railroads
to have the tracks   tear open his heart
like the iron melting in the dragon's teeth.

Let one arm be the walking cane.
Hold it high above your head.
It will lead you to where they are buried.

Which of my faces   flared in the candlelight?
How did I find I was wrong when
I couldn't swallow the sweetness of prayer?

Long ago, I ignored the church
without knowing it was the trance
that kept us together.

The broken *maracas* in the old books
shake for the first words I learned in English,
almost forgot the Spanish   of my spoken fears.

Who powers the gourd of the *maraca*
to roll from cheek to cheek?
As I listened,   I uncovered my last piece of bread.

As I dug for an old sound in the book,
I recited a long list of hope
and missed two   or three words.

Odes to the Family of Spiders

I hide behind the house, hear the cries of my mother looking for me,
summer evening turning black as her anger,
as cold as the side of the house where I crouch,
watch the swamp cooler drip black widow spiders on the ground.

They fall like black marbles, disappear as eyeballs rolling toward the tomb,
huge, fat spiders falling out of the swamp cooler
as my mother shouts my name,
not knowing I hide to descend into the safety of spiders
where I find a web at age four,
bend as small as the spiders carrying secrets the way
I carry what I did wrong into the slippery grass.

I crouch for over an hour, my knees caked in mud,
black widows emerging to surround me,
unaware I would touch them if I knew how the body eats itself,
if I was old enough to know my mother's search
is the unweaving of the strands as they stick to my fingers.

I would touch the spiders if I was sure their bite brought me
closer to the wet puddle of young men where we gather as boys,
learn to crawl toward voices in the dirt,
until it is safe to get up and go back into the quiet house.

*

> Raking soaked yellow leaves,
> I uncover
> three hibernating spiders.
> Looking closer,
> I see they are brown recluses,
> their liquid frozen
> in sleep,
> their slow bodies
> barely moving,

legs vibrating
to come alive.

I must destroy them
before they go
into the house,
worried they could bite
someone.
I think about
how they say
brown recluses
eat your flesh
into a steak-size wound,
collapsing into your body.

I should kill them
before they turn me
into the digging man
who grabs moist ground
to bring everything
back to life,
his body shaking
with cold harvest,
brown recluses wriggling
like small stars

that secretly fell
to burn with
the digger's desire
to cover his tracks
without stepping on them,
as their pointed legs
mark the spot
where he spit,
in agony,
into the boiling sand.

*

Five daddy longlegs on the ceiling
wait for me to turn off the light

so they can move around the bed
as I dream of being surrounded by webs,

a guest of a wise, old poet
with a house built by spiders.

Five of them explore my body as I sleep,
move like miniature ferris wheels

in my dream of being captured and taken
to the corner of the room where I lose

my vision to the sleeping song
of patient spiders,

a poet retired to a forest
of potent recital where I stay ahead

of the daddy longlegs by having short vision,
deep eyes that reach into creeping motion,

a time to hide in the room
under the trees where spiders leave a sign,

a thin, white symbol woven on my snoring head,
its course the thread to another life,

a chance of reaching out
with the bitten, swollen hand.

Never

I never worked on car engines
with my father.
We never saw the mechanics
of the world or shared
a joke about the deep
losses between men.

We never ate a meal together,
just the two of us.
We never identified stars in the sky
as witnesses to our longing,
our wrestling and shuffling to embrace
like drunk bears colliding with trees,
alone in the thick forest of our separate dreams.

Fathers

"*I imagine my father hanging from my feet and my grandfather hanging from the feet of my father. It is all one, and still we will conquer.*"
—Gonzalo Rojas

I look down and we are one,
suspended in the air, headed

toward the moment when we do
the same things, commit the same acts

to save ourselves from the hatred
and awful fear of our fathers,

those sons who came before us
to fuck and settle down

in search of a better life
through hard work and ignorance,

sin and betrayal,
escape and triumph.

I look down and we are hanging
from the same family tree

that bends in the wind of our shame to hide
what we did from our wives and children.

We hang and drift in the clouds
so the great story of our fathers can be told

by the son born to climb the tree, cut the rope,
and watch the bodies fall.

The Energy of Clay

My mother once said,
"When you drink from the jar,
you can taste the desert."
    She looked for grains of dirt,
chips of the inner jar in water.
"Crunch the dirt in your teeth
and you taste the earth."

We drank from the jar,
inhaled the smell of cold water
like an underground spring we dared dig up,
earthy taste of the jar filling us with need
    to go down deeper, settle into the cave
like we had no choice—
our thirst meant we were fated to go under,
never look up at the sky,
always down to the ground where jars sprang
like brown wombs of the mother giving us
the first taste of clay.

    I come up, roll the dirt,
praise the clay for being so pure,
sharper and hotter than the form I tried to shape.
I pound it like the last traveler afraid water
will not help him.

I push my palms together.
The desert emerges from my oozing hands.

The face of my father falls into the plant.
The face of the sweetness of earth takes shape
from the clay ruins.

The desert expands to cover us.
The face of clay melts in the canyons.

Of the family, I know little.
They left to dig where the clay comes up,
alive, perfect for the fingers
where moisture seeps,
obeys the masked hands.

Of my father, he lives in two worlds—
land of the digger and the cave of clay,
territory he never inhabits because
his houses were built from harder ground,
mixture of the bitter cottonwood and the thorn,
formed with the isolation of walls where all fathers,
in their son's clay, lie down to forget.

IV.
The Heat of Arrivals

The Heat of Arrivals

There are ways to take the heat of arrivals,
when the hundred-year old flower opens
in the gray-haired woman
and she forces you to stand in the sun.
There are reasons to love the tongue before it speaks
of the sadness in kissing its own lips,
translating for the children who went blind
when the strangers on horses took them away.
There are fires and notes in the welcoming haze,
the arrival of the bare feet in the hesitant rain,
a migrating witness who brings no crime.

There are ways to mistake the heat of arrivals,
when the brilliant candle kills the field of onions,
becomes the summer when everyone left,
getting out before the moving of the jars.
There is thirst mistaken for the gift of clouds,
generations with lies passed down
to risk apparitions and avoid the cross.

There is music in the heat of suspicion,
the howling of the coyote who follows the road
and keeps pace with the car.

There is nostalgia for the cemetery,
rearranging rusted cans of flowers,
bringing back a shawl and the scent
to begin again.
There is one needle with its glass-stained
membrane embalming the air.

There is time to remove heat from the visitor
who wanted the flower because it was warm,
a sharpness unable to sustain what he brought.
There is no degree to the heat that leaves him

in the hands of the gray-haired woman,
ninety years of an age when the only thing
she couldn't change was the sun
that broke the morning she didn't wake.

Praise the Tortilla, Praise Menudo, Praise Chorizo

For Juan Felipe Herrera

I praise the tortilla in honor of El Panson
who hit me in school every day,
made me see how the bruises on my arms looked
like the brown clouds on my mother's tortillas.
I praise the tortilla because I know they
fly into our hands like eager flesh of the one we love,
soft yearnings we delight in biting as we tear
the tortilla and wipe the plate clean.

> I praise the menudo as the visionary food,
> the *tripa y posole* tight flashes of color we see
> as the red *caldo* smears across our notebooks,
> our lives going down like the empty bowls
> of menudo with the *chili piquin* of our poetic dreams.

I praise the chorizo and smear it across
my face and hands, the dayglow brown of it
painting me with desire to find out why
the chorizo sizzled in the pan and covered the house
with a smell of growing up I will never have again,
the chorizo burrito hot in my hands
when I ran out to play and show the vatos
it was time to cut the chorizo,
tell it like it is before *la manteca* runs
down our chins and drips away.

The Toy

It grew out of the rapid rains,
left at my doorstep   tinged with silver
from past weddings and ceremonies,

resembling a large, antlered animal,
not elk nor moose.
The horns lay in   a muddy heap at my door,

a gift from the toymaker who left it,
months before the Christmas star,
weeks before my birthday.

I lifted it in the rain.
It weighed on my chest and legs like
the trunk of a cottonwood   cut in a storm,

heaving against its victim.
I carried it to the backyard,
laid it in the steaming grass like

an animal sleeping after finding me
                without a weapon,
a gnarled plaything of wood and bone

sinking into flooded ground
so I could bend in the rain,
run my dripping fingers over

        the sharpest part of the toy,
an imperfection of great horns
inviting me to plant it like

the skeleton of a child who created
toys out of limb and roots,
                until he grew too old,

dropped this mass of bark and skin
    before the house of the next boy,
his refusal to dismantle the knotted bulbs.

Late Night Moon

After Galway Kinnell

The moon closes its eyes,
  bends into the eastern territory,
    its frozen music the numb sound
      never granted, a collision opening a passage.

Once more, the rains polish
  my trance with an electric skin
    where lightning hits, allowing the ground to sink.
      The huge space of doubt settles over
        the geometry of what I have been.

Past the imprint of the hours,
  in the moving night sparks,
    there are impossible notions in finding
      the arrow stuck in the rapid eye of my skull.

It hurtles faster as it pierces
  the embers toward what I should have been
    when the moon hit the glass.

*

The night listens.
  These have to be the wages of love,
    knowing too much without taking the clot
      out of the beat, the dance out of the blood.

I close the book, see the photo
  of the "life mask" as the man holds it to the light,
    its closed eyes far from what he knows,
      eyelids like the ones I opened
        when I molded the mask out of wood.

*

January moons continue to fade.
  The night rhymes with the hush I hate.
    The moon releases the man and the woman
      so they have another night to believe in each other,
        another late moon over their first quiet house.

I go to the window and see how the cold
  reminds me of the respected dead hanging from trees
    like bodies of natives burned by custom,
      as if this calling stirs sound in this sleeping house,

as if I know what it means to suspend belief
  from the great tree I wish would rain
    over my wife and my house to protect us.

I want to slip around the tree, a lover wanting
  the limbs to unfasten a role he accepted
    when moonlight was metal on his arms.

Moonlight was the kiss the two of them missed,
  knowing the glow was meant to destroy their doubts,
    a reminder this arc measures how far they go
      as the moon rocks them past sleep.

When the paws enter the house,
  my eyes close to avoid the fire that follows,
    a white globe hurting in my shoulder blade
      as I turn and hold her, admitting the bodies

that don't know what the moon does to them
  are part of the motions and tides
    where I wake to begin.

Years Later

Winter will come to slap
stupidity out of our brains.
We will train ourselves in the art
of composing a solid,
tragic, humorous pain.
Afraid to move, we raise
our own flock of birds.

Under our porches, old friends
turn away to say
something we can't believe.
Perhaps the porch squeaks with the weight.
Perhaps we will hate something
moving in the dark.

There are eight names for greed,
six words for love.

Inside our muffled days,
four words in a cry for help.

Winter allows one embrace,
one hug between the lovers and the storm.

Inside the snowflakes,
our thoughts are preserved
in patterns of lace.
Inside the cold,
a senseless loss for words
precedes the arrival
of someone, frostbitten,
crossing the road.

The Magnets

On turning forty

They draw me closer like the hands
of one grandmother I kissed upon
visiting her in the barrio.
The magnets make me look at my waist,
wonder why the ache is in the street,
houses giving off stinking air,
a magnetic field collecting old newspapers,
broken-down cars, alleys where
the drummer cowers before he beats
on his bag of beer cans.

I visit the irrigation canal that
churns green and flows beyond the streets,
wait for the alligator to swim by,
the one released from the plaza long ago.
I feel the pull toward the mongrel dog,
the clicking of the magnets in the church,
an attraction for open doorways.

*

I remove the magnet from my neck,
a medal of a denied saint.
It eases the pull toward the barbed-wire fence.
I will never witness the migration of bats again,
stand at the entrance of the caverns
as bats shoot out of the opening,
the evening bristling with their intelligence,
the black cloud a mass of sound.

The sky bruises against the horizon
of yucca plants surrounding
the cavern, erect as magnets,

miles of yucca encircling the poles
as if their silhouettes protect
the tunnel, clear it of wind
that pulls me into the hole.

*

He tells me to believe what I have seen.
He insists magnetic force comes from the blade,
the woman wanting us to keep something for her.
He says magnets are missing metals
from an underground wound,
a husband's wrist broken by a slammed car hood,
loyal dance of an old couple watching the street.

He says tortillas and menudo sometimes attract flies.
He learned red chili kills all life.
He insists magnets let him sleep fulfilled,
delicious food he fixes
long after his wife has died.
He says magnets get stronger when he peels
the pods to find no difference
in the seeds of hunger and the seeds of love.

*

I climb the rocks because the minerals are there.
I climb to where I buried the sea shell,
rusted can, and pencil twenty-eight years ago.
I climb the rocks because I am allowed one mountain.
I climb to readjust the magnets,
stand and look down.
I clear my chest of a fist never encountered up here.
I climb to set my foot on the humming slab.
I climb to survive when I touch my heart.
I climb before deciding I must bend and dig.

Was Federico García Lorca Lonely
in New York?

Was Federico García Lorca lonely in New York?
Did he climb the streets like a statue of rock
rebelling against the sculptor, turning on
his creator to take the chisel out of his hands?

Was Federico crying in New York?
Did he wipe his tears with hands holding oranges
whose juice punishes all men of crippled hope,
or did he stare at the harbor and wait for the gulls
to screech into blinding stars shooting across
immigration lines, bread lines of people
too hungry to drink their cups of blood?

Was García Lorca able to sleep in New York?
Did he wake above the city blocks to identify
the makers of brick and mortar, builders of slums,
ghosts of crowded rooms, doors of troubled sleep?

Did Lorca slash the duende in New York?
Did he find the black guitar in the ashes
raining over the Brooklyn Bridge,
or meet the many-colored gypsy in the alley
of singing flames, the barrio of wailing love
and the forgotten tambourine?

Was Federico searching for something in New York?
Did Spain turn into a wolf hunting for him
as he looked for the woman of flowers in Central Park,
search for the child in the fish markets of Harlem,
go after the crowds of people everywhere?

Did García Lorca go crazy in New York?
Were his eyes drilling the heart of the subways
to find a place to hide his poems?
Before leaving, did he dance the steps of death
in recognition of firing squads lining up?

Did Lorca run toward the lights
of the harbor of false liberty?
Did he finally get out of the way,
or was he carried to the moon by the thousands
of pigeons fleeing the future city?

These Days

These years the border closes,
mojados sent back to be found as bodies in the river,
or the cut-off head hanging in the tree.
The gang in the barrio where I work sprays
graffiti on my office door, symbols I don't understand.
The English and Spanish don't belong to me.
They vibrate in drive-by shootings,
boys gasping with laughter and the gun,
betting on who will get shot or dance in prison.

Inside a mountain,
a man gets up and wonders what happened to
the *cuento* passed to him about madness
of a family who fled here, building a stone bridge
to hold water that saved them, made their corn grow.
Water seeps into the man's ears when he lies down.
It trickles into the room where he grows old,
water weeping out of the saguaro so he can cup his hands.

The hills contain graves of Mejicanos,
the rumor my father's ancestors were throat-cutting thieves
buried without markers on their graves.
I read about the psychic in the Alamo who encountered
spirits of Mejicanos forced into Santa Ana's army to die.
He contacts Bernardo y Juan Vargas, brothers trapped
156 years as tourists step on them,
soldiers revealing they want to rest in peace.
The psychic asks if the ghost of John Wayne dwells here.
The brothers tell him Wayne wanders among the dead,
never speaks because he can't find
the spirits of the Texas heroes.

I wave to the gang member we hired
to paint a mural on our center wall,
his arms finishing the blue and yellow feathers

on the Aztec face he created,
showing me how the man trapped in the mountain
can find his way out when I enter the old house to find
he is a muralist mixing color from
the burned mirrors under our familiar floors.

"I Haven't Any Bread and Will Live a Long Life"

—*Attila Jozsef*

There is nothing left
on the soles of my shoes.
I walked to believe
there was time to think,
demand I find something new
before I drift away from my first beliefs,
go against the ghost coming out
of my shoes to disappear
into the trees like someone I hated.

I wanted to believe the poor ones
in the colonias of El Paso knew I lived there,
once, without bread or water to feed anyone,
without bowls of beans and water I grew allergic to.
I buried that meal beyond their reach,
hid it in the territory they can't inhabit,
dig it up every time I see myself going back.

Something sacred is taught
when we repossess neighborhoods,
turn them into safe places to walk
before we settle into the life of the bare foot,
the kiss of sole that blisters us
if we step hard enough,
if we enter like a presence no one sees,
but knows is there by the footprints
shimmering over the hot ground.

Easter Sunday 1988, the Grand Canyon, Arizona

Bodies are resurrected
as the whole earth opens
to show how far we must fall
to keep falling,
how deeply we must fear the savage god
that tears the distance
into red miles of a planet
we will never reach,
the other side of fear
we will never climb because
the trail to the bottom leads
to the tomb of the river
where the earth eats itself,

feeds upon the river that devours the river
until we rise in our own space
to float miles across a canyon
that is not a landscape,
but remains of a great prayer
whose chant cut hundreds of miles of rock
into one big tomb where our bodies
start falling again, descend
to the bottom of inner atmospheres,
where gravity grabs us off the rim,
the river rising to meet us
the last thing we ever see.

The Owl's Mask

What happened to the god who removed it?
Where did he fall after the battle?
How many owls hid in the saguaro
when their faces were suddenly revealed
by a stroke of lightning?

In the pushy dream,
the wings act like brothers
wrapping themselves around you,
frightening you by lifting
a weight across the desert.

With a quick blinking,
the god returns to replace
huge eyes with white vision,
sharp pools of high patience

as the owl is taken toward
the sanctuary of wings
where faces of birds
are the eyes of those who
followed you across the sands,

alighting in your path to embed
one talon in your forehead,
pass its mask from mind to thought,
making sure you know when
to let go from great heights.

Acknowledgments

The author would like to thank the editors and publishers of the following journals, anthologies, and chapbooks where some of the poems first appeared.

After Aztlan: Latino Poets in the Nineties (David R. Godine Publishers): "The Sustenance," "Rattlesnake Dance, Coronado Hills, 1966," "Three Snakes, Strawberry Canyon, Berkeley," "Snakeskin (*A Dream*)";

Chariton Review: "Was Federico García Lorca Lonely in New York?";

Cincinnati Poetry Review: "Years Later";

Colorado Review: "The Magnets," "Snakeskin: A Dream," "Four Times The Feast," "Song For The Lizard Painted on the Plate";

Cutbank: "Memory of the Hand";

Grounded in Stone and Sky: An Anthology of Arizona Writing (University of Arizona Press): "Easter Sunday 1988, Grand Canyon, Arizona";

Hispanic American Literature & Art For Young People (Harry N. Abrams, Inc.): "The Energy of Clay";

Kenyon Review: "How?" "The Heat of Arrivals";

Mangrove: "In Peru, the Quechans Have a Thousand Words for Potato";

Massachusetts Review: "These Days";

Mid-American Review: "Fathers";

New Chicano Writing #1 (University of Arizona Press): "The Energy of Clay," "The Blue Snake," "Homage to Lucian Blaga";

Northern Lights: "The Owl's Mask";

Paper Dance: Latino Poets for the New Millennium (Persea Books): "Homage to Lucian Blaga," "The Snakes as a Gift for My Aching Shoulder";

Permafrost: "I Haven't Any Bread and Will Live a Long Life";

Prairie Schooner: "The Grandfather" "Three Snakes, Strawberry Canyon, Berkeley";

Puerto Del Sol: "Praise the Tortilla, Praise Menudo, Praise Chorizo";

RE: Arts & Letters: "The Cathedral of My Father";

Sierra Club Desert Reader (Sierra Club Books): "Easter Sunday 1988, Grand Canyon, Arizona";

Sounds from the Thorn (Long Hand Press): "The Eagles in the Ashes," "The Snake in Winter," "The Blue Snake," "Easter Sunday 1988, Grand Canyon, Arizona";

South Florida Poetry Review: "Never";

Taos Review: "The Owl's Mask";

The Forgotten Language: Contemporary Poets & Nature (Gibbs Smith Publishers): "Easter Sunday 1988, Grand Canyon, Arizona";

Tracks in the Snow: Essays by Colorado Poets (Mesilla Press): "Indian Petroglyphs, Red Desert, Wyoming";

Unsettling America: Race & Ethnicity in Contemporary American Poetry (William R. Morrow): "Praise the Tortilla, Praise Menudo, Praise Chorizo."

I would like to thank The Colorado Council on the Arts for a Creative Fellowship in Literature, which helped in finding time to complete the early poems in this book. Some of these poems appeared in a letter-press limited edition as part of a Book Arts collaboration with printmaker Leslie Koptcho and typographer Rod Mills, a project funded by The City of San Antonio Department of Arts & Cultural Affairs.

For their early influence during my years in El Paso, I thank Robert Burlingame and the late Raymond Carver, two writers and teachers whose quiet voices were the most powerful. My years in Colorado, where most of these poems were written, could not have been rich with poetry without the friendship and support of Phil Woods, Tom Parson, George Kalamaras, Betty Chancellor, and Tom and Marilyn Auer. In San Antonio and San Marcos I am indebted to Jesse Cardona, Cynthia Harper, Kathleen Pierce, and Bob Randolph for helping me see my work differently after so many years away from the desert. I thank my wife Ida for her meticulous assistance with the manuscript and for knowing what it takes.

About the Author

Ray Gonzalez is a poet, essayist, and editor born in El Paso, Texas. He is the author of *Memory Fever: A Journey Beyond El Paso del Norte* (Broken Moon Press, 1993), a memoir about growing up in the Southwest. He was educated at The University of Texas at El Paso and Southwest State University, where he received an MFA in Creative Writing. He is the author of two earlier books of poetry: *From the Restless Roots* (Arte Publico Press, 1985) and *Twilights and Chants* (James Andrews & Co., 1987). He is the editor of sixteen anthologies, most recently *Currents From the Dancing River: Contemporary Latino Essays, Fiction, and Poetry* (Harcourt Brace, 1994) and *Muy Macho: Latino Men Confront Their Manhood* (Anchor / Doubleday, 1996). He has served as Poetry Editor of *The Bloomsbury Review*, a book review magazine in Denver, for fifteen years. Among his awards are a 1987 Four Corners Book Award for *Twilights and Chants*, a 1988 Colorado Governor's Award for Excellence in the Arts, and a 1993 Before Columbus Foundation Book Award for Excellence in Editing. He is assistant professor of English and Latin American Studies at the University of Illinois in Chicago.

BOA EDITIONS, LTD.: AMERICAN POETS CONTINUUM SERIES

0058